Hut
Hutchinson, Emily
Leopoldo Alas : stories /

34028059763939
MM ocm32128758

W9-DBV-034
HARRIS COUNTY PUBLIC LIBRARY

LAKE CLASSICS

Great Short Stories from Around the World I

Leopoldo ALAS

Stories retold by Emily Hutchinson
Illustrated by James Balkovek

LAKE EDUCATION
Belmont, California

LAKE CLASSICS

Great American Short Stories I

Washington Irving, Nathaniel Hawthorne, Mark Twain, Bret Harte, Edgar Allan Poe, Kate Chopin, Willa Cather, Sarah Orne Jewett, Sherwood Anderson, Charles W. Chesnutt

Great American Short Stories II

Herman Melville, Stephen Crane, Ambrose Bierce, Jack London, Edith Wharton, Charlotte Perkins Gilman, Frank R. Stockton, Hamlin Garland, O. Henry, Richard Harding Davis

Great British and Irish Short Stories I

Arthur Conan Doyle, Saki (H. H. Munro), Rudyard Kipling, Katherine Mansfield, Thomas Hardy, E. M. Forster, Robert Louis Stevenson, H. G. Wells, John Galsworthy, James Joyce

Great Short Stories from Around the World I

Guy de Maupassant, Anton Chekhov, Leo Tolstoy, Selma Lagerlöf, Alphonse Daudet, Mori Ogwai, Leopoldo Alas, Rabindranath Tagore, Fyodor Dostoevsky, Honoré de Balzac

Cover and Text Designer: Diann Abbott

Copyright © 1994 by Lake Education, a division of Lake Publishing Company, 500 Harbor Blvd., Belmont, CA 94002. All rights reserved. No part of this book may be reproduced by any means, transmitted, or translated into a machine language without written permission from the publisher.

Library of Congress Catalog Number: 94-075346
ISBN 1-56103-045-7
Printed in the United States of America
1 9 8 7 6 5 4 3 2

CONTENTS

❦ Lake Classic Short Stories ❧

"The universe is made of stories, not atoms."
—Muriel Rukeyser

"The story's about you."
—Horace

Everyone loves a good story. It is hard to think of a friendlier introduction to classic literature. For one thing, short stories are *short*—quick to get into and easy to finish. Of all the literary forms, the short story is the least intimidating and the most approachable.

Great literature is an important part of our human heritage. In the belief that this heritage belongs to everyone, *Lake Classic Short Stories* are adapted for today's readers. Lengthy sentences and paragraphs are shortened. Archaic words are replaced. Modern punctuation and spellings are used. Many of the longer stories are abridged. In all the stories, painstaking care has been taken to preserve the author's unique voice.

Lake Classic Short Stories have something for everyone. The hundreds of stories in the collection cover a broad terrain of themes, story types, and styles. Literary merit was a deciding factor in story selection. But no story was included unless it was as enjoyable as it was instructive. And special priority was given to stories that shine light on the human condition.

Each book in the *Lake Classic Short Stories* is devoted to the work of a single author. Little-known stories of merit are included with famous old favorites. Taken as a whole, the collected authors and stories make up a rich and diverse sampler of the story-teller's art.

Lake Classic Short Stories guarantee a great reading experience. Readers who look for common interests, concerns, and experiences are sure to find them. Readers who bring their own gifts of perception and appreciation to the stories will be doubly rewarded.

❧ Leopoldo Alas ❧
(1852–1901)

About the Author

Leopoldo Alas, better known by his pen name "Clarín," was born in Zamora, Spain. Although his father was a provincial governor, the family was far from wealthy. Young Leopoldo was a talented student. He wrote his first serious play when he was only 13. At 17 he graduated from college with honors.

While he was still a teenager, Alas went to Madrid to study law. His political activities there made him some powerful enemies. Twice he was challenged to fight a duel for his stinging attacks on the government.

Alas's first short stories were published in 1877 when he was 25. In the same year he earned his Doctor of Laws degree. After that he worked as a college professor as well as a writer.

Some 15 years later, two collections of his short stories were published. These established his reputation as a great writer of short fiction.

Alas's novel *La Regenta* is considered one of the major works of European fiction in the 19th century. It tells a realistic story of life in the Spanish provinces. Among the Spanish writers of his day, Alas was very modern. Like the French writers, he used naturalism and psychological insight to make his characters come alive on the page.

As an occasional journalist, Alas continued to fight for his political beliefs. In his newspaper articles, the poetic Alas spoke in harsh, biting language. At times, only the help of his friends kept him out of serious difficulties with the government.

Alas died at 49. Even in his lifetime he was highly regarded. The great novelist Azorin said this of him: "Clarin is one of those writers to whom the learned always turn."

Doña Berta

Would you give up personal happiness for the sake of family honor? The proud Rondaliego family has demanded just that from Doña Berta. Now she has one last chance to salvage her *own* pride.

BERTA FOUND THE WOUNDED CAPTAIN AT THE GATE.

Doña Berta

There is a spot in northern Spain that neither the Romans nor the Moors ever reached. This quiet green hideaway is the home of Doña Berta de Rondaliego. The land has been in her family for generations. The soil here is forever soft with lush, fresh grass. The area is called Zaornín, and the huge valley is called Susacasa. In the valley is a large meadow called Aren.

A tree-lined stream borders one side of the meadow. The stream does not have a name, for it is very small. But the Rondaliego family has always called it "the river." Their neighbors, just to be mean and disrespectful, like to call it "the drip."

Doña Berta doesn't like it when her neighbors cross the river. For one thing, they insult the river by crossing it without using a bridge. But even worse, they trample on the ground. Their rude feet crush the beautiful wild flowers and kill the grass.

Beyond the stream is a field of corn. When the stalks grow, their leaves make the field look like a green sea blown by the breezes. On the other side of that sea is the "mansion." In truth it is a not very large white house. This is the Rondaliego home.

Attached to the main house is a chapel. There is also a storehouse for grain nearby. And there is a pigeon roost and a little hut that serves as a farmhouse. Together, these buildings and the land are called Posadorio.

Doña Berta and her servant, Sabelona, live alone in the "mansion." With them lives "the cat." Like "the river," the cat has no name because it is the only one thereabouts. The old farmhouse is where the caretaker lives. His daughter and their servant live there as well. The servant is a different one every few days. That is because the caretaker has such a bad temper. He fires people for the smallest things.

The estate is quite run down. But even if it were in good shape, it would not be worth much. The green, fresh-looking land is not really first class. It produces almost nothing. This explains why Doña Berta is so poor.

Of course, she imagines that she is special because of her old family background. And the Rondaliegos were never friendly with their neighbors. In fact, they looked down on them. They called them "riffraff" and "rabble."

At Doña Berta's house, bread is baked every five or six days. This task takes more muscle than Doña Berta and Sabelona have together. They need the help of the caretaker's daughter.

But Doña Berta and Sabelona do all

their own spinning. And they wash their own clothes. As soon as the wash comes back from the river, they spread it out on the grass to dry. Doña Berta loves to look out on the meadow when the wash is drying there. Sometimes she wishes she had the hands of a giant—each hand a mile long. Then she could stroke the meadow's back, just as she does her cat's.

The district called Zaornín is not on the way to anywhere. Highways and trains do not go by there. "This is the tip end of the world," says Doña Berta. Of course, she has some strange ideas about geography. But she has said this to her ever-faithful servant many times. Sabelona has been with the Rondaliego family since she was 10. Now the two old women are in their 70s.

"Neither the Moors nor the Romans have ever come here!" says Doña Berta. She does not really know how long ago the Moslem and Roman periods in Spain were. When someone once told her that the French never came there either, she just shrugged. It was as if she were saying, "Well, that's all included in the Moors and the Romans." The fact was that the Moors and the Romans had come to be a symbol to Doña Berta. They stood for everything that was strange, foreign, and dangerous.

The Rondaliego family was made up of four brothers and one sister, Berta. Their parents had died when they were children. The oldest son, Don Claudio, had acted as father to the rest.

The Rondaliegos were all good, kind people. But their works of charity were done from afar. They feared the common people, even though they loved them as brothers in Christ. They just didn't want to have anything to do with them.

Several generations back, a young Rondaliego had been found dead in a forest near Posadorio. It was thought that he had been murdered by a local villager. Since then, the whole family was afraid of the villagers, even when giving out charity. The townsfolk received their gifts with thanks. But then they joked behind their backs. They showed their disrespect whenever they could.

Local laws were passed that taxed the Rondaliegos at a higher rate than everyone else. At the same time, police protection within the limits of Zaornín was stopped. So when fruit, hay, firewood, and such were stolen, the guilty parties were never caught.

"Fine!" the owners of Posadorio would say to themselves. "The people, the common villagers, don't like us. But we don't like them either. So be it." Still, they gave whatever they could to the poor people of the area.

All the brothers of the family were bachelors. Their most prized possession was their honor. And that honor, that purity, came to rest in Berta, their only sister. But Berta was different from her brothers. She had inside of her a tenderness that her brothers lacked. Never would her brothers have guessed it. A roaring flame of fantasy and emotion lived right there in Posadorio!

Not even after the "misfortune" did they guess the cause. Instead, they blamed chance, the moment, and treachery. All of these, of course, were partly to blame. But the brothers never thought of love. They never dreamed of a heart that melts when it nears the fire it adores. The misfortune came about because Berta had fallen in love. And she had done so with all of the eagerness in her soul.

The story was quite simple. Along came "the Captain," a soldier in Queen Cristina's armies. The poor man had been wounded. He fell right at the gate of the Rondaliego home. When Berta came out, she saw the blood, the uniform, and a pair of gentle blue eyes. The eyes seemed to be begging for mercy—maybe even for love. She took the poor man in and hid him in the chapel.

She didn't tell her brothers right away, for they were Carlists, as she was. They might turn the man over to their own side, as a prisoner of war. But after thinking it over, she finally decided to tell her brothers her secret. They approved of what she had done. The wounded man was moved to the best feather bed in the house. The whole family kept the matter quiet. When the Carlist troops passed by, they never dreamed that one of their enemies was hidden in an upstairs bedroom.

For two months, Berta took care of the Captain all by herself. She was attracted to him from the first day. Her brothers let her nurse him. They didn't know she was falling in love with him. They expected that all her affection would disappear as soon as he was well enough to leave.

Soon the Captain was well enough to stroll around the garden. From then on, a friendship grew between Berta's brothers and the Captain. The Captain was warm and funny. He told wonderful stories. He liked people, and people liked him. Soon he was organizing chess matches and card games. He read aloud in a beautiful voice after supper.

Finally the day came when the Captain felt that he must return to his place at the front. He said that his heart would remain behind, with Berta—but he really had to leave. The brothers would not hear of it. The longer he stayed, they said, the better he would repay them for helping him. The real reason, of course, was that they enjoyed his company so much.

The Captain let himself be talked into it. He stayed in Posadorio longer than he should have. The truth was that he was falling in love with Berta, as she already had with him. The brothers were blind to what was happening. One day they went hunting, leaving the Captain and Berta home alone.

While the brothers were gone, the Captain threw himself at Berta's feet. She, who knew nothing about such things, burst into tears. When his flaming kiss burned her lips and her heart, all she could do was cry. She didn't lose her virtue that day. That happened later on, in the garden. It was at twilight, under a laurel tree that smelled as sweet as paradise.

Later, the Captain promised to return as soon as possible. Then he would ask her brothers for her hand in marriage. He said that he would have to quit the army. He knew that her brothers would never let her marry an officer of the enemy army.

Berta was completely innocent. She knew that something serious had happened. But she didn't think that it was anything terrible. It wasn't that she was afraid to tell her brothers. She kept the incident in the garden to herself for the sweet warmth of its mystery.

All she knew was what the Captain said: *he would come back and marry her.* That was fine. As for happiness—she already had it locked in her heart. She would wait 100 years if she had to. The Captain said he would avoid danger like a coward. He was returning to the front just to do his job. He would do everything possible to save his own skin. Now his life was no longer his own. It belonged to Berta's honor.

But things didn't quite work out that way. This brave Captain had been happy only twice in his life. On those two occasions, he had caused a terrible misfortune and started a luckless life. One evening, he heard the call of war's hymn. Death, like a great love, called him from the trench. His soldiers looked to him for his example—and he gave it to them. On that night he offered up his body to the bullets and his soul to God.

The Rondaliego brothers never heard from him again. Neither did Berta. She didn't know that her heart's choice had been unable to come back. The Captain had left the day after promising to marry Berta. Nobody suspected the shame he left behind. But then the unlucky girl's pregnancy started to become apparent.

Berta began to realize her sin through its punishment. Her son was snatched from her. Then her brothers left her alone in Posadorio with Sabelona and some other servants. They divided up all the money they had inherited. Berta was given Posadorio and all the surrounding land along with her share of the money. Part of her punishment was to live in the place where she had dishonored the family name. There, she would be more alone than in any other place.

Many long years passed before the Rondaliegos were able to forget, if not to forgive. Two of the brothers died in the war soon after. The other two fought in the war but lived to be old men. As they grew older, they would sometimes visit Berta. Back they would come to the "place of dishonor"—but they no longer called it that. Berta had forgiven herself too, almost without thinking about it.

But if Berta had begun to forgive her own sin, she never forgave her brothers for the "theft" of her son. When she was young, it almost seemed like a fair punishment. But as she grew older, she could pardon neither her brothers nor herself. "I should have protested. I should have demanded the right to keep my son. I should have looked for him at any cost. I should not have believed my brothers when they said he died."

Finally it occurred to Berta that she might be able to find out where her son was. But it was already too late. He had vanished from sight. Her brothers had erased all possible means of finding him. At first, they had lied to Berta about the poor child's death in order to punish her. Later, they lied so that she would not resent them for her grief.

Berta's last two brothers died in Posadorio two years apart. Berta did not dare to ask the first one, her oldest brother, about her son. At the time of his death, she thought about it as she looked into his eyes. She had the feeling that he was thinking about it, too. But he said nothing. Shortly after he died, she gently closed those eyes that had held her deepest secret.

Only two years after that, her only remaining brother was breathing his last. Berta was about to be left alone in the world. She threw herself on the thin chest of the dying man. She asked him about her son. "Did he die? Did he really die? Are you quite sure? Swear to me, Agustín." And Agustín looked up at his sister. But he could no longer see her, and his last tear fell as he died.

Then Berta was left alone with Sabelona and the cat. She began to age quickly. In just a year or two, she became a skinny, yellowed old woman—she, who once was so fair and round! And she became hard of hearing.

Now she came and went up and down the cornfield, giving orders to sow the lands and trim the trees. But in the middle of all this activity, she would look over her lonely land. Sad memories would wash over her. She thought of her Captain and her son—who had died or disappeared! Then the poor old woman would cry for her child. She had not seen him for 50 years! As she wept for her son, she blamed the world, fate, her brothers, and herself.

One August afternoon, Doña Berta was walking by herself at the far end of her garden. She was near the forest of oaks, firs, and chestnut trees. For some reason she had an urge to go out into the forest. She wanted to wander up the hill. Such an idea had not occurred to her for years. But right at that moment she wanted some adventure, some daring.

When she was young, how many times had she stood by that gate? How many times had she dreamed that something wonderful would come to her through it? Later, when she was waiting for her Captain who never returned, she watched for him through that gate. Now she turned the key in the lock, lifted the latch, and went out into the woods.

After a few steps, she heard a noise. The sound was very close. Suddenly, she saw before her a handsome young man of about 30 or 35. He was dark, strong, and he wore a beard. He was dressed in fine clothes. In fact, he appeared to be a young gentleman. He was carrying a box that hung from a strap around his shoulder.

The two stood looking at each other in silence. At last Doña Berta realized that the man was greeting her. Without hearing him, she answered by bowing her head.

She wasn't afraid. Why should she be? But she was surprised and a little bit annoyed. What was this strange man doing here? After all, Susacasa wasn't on the way to anywhere. It offended her that he should be on her land. She told him that she owned everything he saw there. And what about him? Who was he? What was he doing here?

For a few minutes the young man spoke gently to her. Doña Berta found out that he was a famous artist. His latest painting was hanging in Madrid. He said that half of Spain was admiring it. But while everyone was praising his work, he had decided to get away. That is why he was wandering through the valleys and woods.

The young man told her that he was studying the green shades of the earth and the grays of the sky. He said that he knew all the secrets of the natural beauty of the coast. Doña Berta thought that he had been more daring than either the Romans or the Moors! He had reached the forest of Zaornín and then come to the woods of Susacasa itself! To her, this was like getting to the heart of the mystery.

"Do you like it here?" Doña Berta asked.

"Yes, madam, very much," said the painter. Under his breath, he added, "And I like you, too—you wonderful old woman! You are a living antique."

It was quite true that the artist was delighted. Seeing Doña Berta helped him understand the setting better. This small person seemed "full of outlines," even in her thinness. Her "colors" were those of wax, tobacco, and ashes. Her skin was wax, her hair was ashes, and her eyes and clothing were tobacco.

For quite some time, Doña Berta had been choosing dresses and shawls the color of dead leaves. Her hair had dried out to a shade that was not quite the white of silver. Instead, it seemed like the faded remains of its former color. It was like the rose pink of dusk on long summer days.

To the painter, Doña Berta seemed to be a copy of a small ivory statue. She looked like a carving on a fancy fan. He thought that she must smell of sandalwood.

Doña Berta offered the artist some chocolate and fruit. They ate in the garden, under a laurel tree. They talked for a long time. He tried to keep the talk away from himself. His interest was only in her. But finally, he forgot his "study" of her. Then he began to talk about himself. He told her his life story. To Doña Berta it unfolded like a series of dreams and pictures.

The artist said that he had once painted a girl he loved in the setting of a fountain. Seeing the painting, the public had also fallen in love with her. He had returned to that town in the spring, wanting to marry her. But he found her ill and dying. Talking about this was making him very sad. Trying to change the subject, he asked Doña Berta if *she* had ever had a great love in her life.

Doña Berta looked at the handsome young artist. She felt her heart fill up with her dead youth. It was as if her own dear love were there! She decided to tell the artist about her Captain without telling him all the details. But Doña Berta was not used to hiding the truth. She told the story in such a way that the artist could fill in the missing parts. When her story was ended, he was able to figure out everything that had happened to her.

The old woman remained silent for a moment. Then she asked the artist what he thought. Had the Captain betrayed her or had he died in the war? Based on what she had said about the Captain's character, the artist had an answer. He said that her lover had not returned— *because he could not*.

"Your Captain did not come back because he died as a hero," said the artist. "And here is where our stories meet. Listen, and you will know what I mean! My painting, which I told you about earlier, is receiving much praise. The subject of that painting is also a Captain. In my heart, I feel that your Captain acted just as mine did. You might find the story of 'my' Captain interesting.

"Some years ago, I was not as well known as I am now. I needed some money. I took a job with a newspaper and was assigned to make sketches of Spanish life. The newspaper especially wanted sketches of the war. Wanting to do a portrait of a hero, I decided to go off to the battlefields in the north. I wanted to see real fighting close up. I thought that if I myself were in danger, I could better understand the feeling. This understanding would help me paint a better portrait.

"Well, during that war, I met 'my' Captain. He knew what I wanted to see so he broke some military rules. He let me go places where only soldiers were allowed to go. My Captain was a brave man and a gambler. He played so well and was so honorable that gambling seemed almost a virtue in him. Somehow it gave him the chance to show many of his good qualities. One day I spoke to him about his daring and bravery.

"'I am not daring, or even brave,' he said. 'In fact, I must act almost like a coward. That is, I have to be careful about risking my life. My life is not mine, you see. It belongs to someone I owe money to. Not long ago, a friend of mine stopped me from killing myself. For the first time in my life, I had gambled more than I owned. I had lost more than I could pay back. Rather than lose my honor, I decided to end my life. Then my friend surprised me in my moment of despair. He gave me the money to pay my debt.

"'After I had paid the money, he said that his honor was in my hands. He said that the money he had given me wasn't really his—that someday he would have to give it back. If he didn't return the money, he would lose his good name.

"'My friend told me to stay alive so that I could help him pay the money back. The honor of two people, then, came to depend on my life. And so, Mr. Artist, I try to avoid combat. As soon as possible, I shall leave the army—but only when I can do so with honor. Until then, I must be very careful.'

"That, my dear lady, is what my Captain told me. On the following day, I noticed that he did not take any foolish chances in battle. But the weeks passed. There was more fighting. Again he began to take daring risks. At last, there came 'the day of my picture.'"

The painter stopped. He took a deep breath. He wanted to remember the moment, as it had happened in real life. Doña Berta was fascinated. She took this time to thank the artist. He had been shouting so that she could hear every word. Then the artist continued on with his story.

"It was a gray, cold day. An important battle was at a turning point. Now the soldiers must either run away or be heroes. They were all about to run, when the gambler became a hero. He threw himself into a sure death—just as he would bet his whole fortune on one card! He took many of his men with him into death and glory.

"That man's act was extraordinary," said the artist. "The look on his face was different from that of any hero in any painting ever done. His eyes showed terrible pain, sorrow, and regret. His forehead, his mouth, and his arms all added to the effect. It was clear that he was facing death as a true hero. Below him and in the distance, other soldiers were hanging back in fear and doubt.

"Oh, Doña Berta, you should see my painting! The public and the critics have fallen in love with my Captain. Everyone has a different way of looking at the painting. But everyone sees the Captain as the best part of the picture. They admire the painting without understanding it.

"Only *I* know the secret of the painting. It shows, dear lady, the real truth about that man who died in battle. The rest of us had to run away, finally. His brave act was wasted. But my painting keeps the memory of him alive. What the world will not know is that my Captain died breaking his word. After all—he had promised not to look for danger."

"That's how *mine* died!" exclaimed Doña Berta. "Yes, my heart shouts to me that my Captain also left me for a death of glory."

Then Doña Berta dropped into her chair and cried. She cried with such despair that the painter was amazed. It seemed that right before him was a statue of history. Yet how could a statue cry about forgotten heroes, joys, and sorrows?

A cold breeze blew by. The old woman stood up and signaled to the painter that he should follow her. They returned to the house. Doña Berta lay down on the couch and kept on crying. When she finally stopped, night was falling.

At last she stood up and wiped her tears away with her thin fingers. Then she said, "My friend, it is now too late for you to find a place to stay. Even though people may talk, you will have to have dinner and spend the night in Posadorio." The artist accepted gladly.

The next day, after making some sketches of Doña Berta, the artist left. Once again, Doña Berta was left alone with her thoughts. Yet, how different her thoughts were now! Of course, her Captain had not returned because he *could not*. He had not been a scoundrel, as her brothers used to say. He had been a hero. Yes, just like the other one—the painter's Captain.

Then her thoughts turned to her son. "Oh, there is nowhere I wouldn't go for my son—dead or alive! What wouldn't I give just to know what became of him! But why is it that in my mind I always see him dead? Why do I never see his open arms?"

Doña Berta was thinking about these things one day. She was surprised when a messenger brought her a package from the artist. Inside, there were two paintings. One was of Doña Berta herself. The other one had the words "My Captain" printed at the bottom. It only showed his head. But when Doña Berta saw that face, she let out a cry of surprise. The Captain of the artist was also hers! The face looked almost exactly like that of the Captain she rememberd so well.

Sabelona came in the room to call Doña Berta. She found the old woman almost ready to faint. All Doña Berta said was, "I don't feel well." She let Sabelona put her to bed. When the doctor came, he couldn't find anything wrong. "It's just old age," he said.

Within three days, Doña Berta was up, more active than ever. Sabelona was surprised when Doña Berta sent off a letter by messenger. To whom could she be writing? Whatever could there be in the outside world that Doña Berta would care about?

The messenger came back four days later. He said that no one at that address knew where the painter was. It might be some time before the letter could be delivered. They would have to wait until the painter returned. Weeks went by, and Doña Berta kept waiting for an answer. Now she could hardly remember what she had said in the letter.

All she could remember was that she had told him the story of her "sin." She had begged him for more information about "his Captain." What was his name? Who was he? Where did he come from? What about his family?

And she also wanted to know the name of the person he had owed money to. She wanted to find that person. And finally, she asked the artist about the painting. Did he still own it, or was it already sold? How much would it cost? Perhaps she could sell everything she owned and pay the Captain's creditor. Would she still be able to buy the painting?

Doña Berta wasn't sure how she had worded these questions. She was sure only that she would never turn back. She had made up her mind to go through with it. Yes, she *wanted* to pay her son's debt.

She *wanted* to buy the picture that showed her son as a hero.

She wasn't sure how much she would get if she sold Susacasa, Posadorio, and Aren. And she didn't know how big her son's debt was. She didn't know how much the painting would cost. But it didn't matter. She would find out.

Her reasons were simple. She had never given her son anything while he was alive. Now that she had "found" him, she wanted to give him everything.

Even though he was dead, her son's honor was her honor. What he owed, she owed. She wanted to pay his debt, even if it cost her everything. And if she still had enough to buy the painting, she would—even if she starved to death.

A few months went by without an answer to her letter. So Doña Berta decided to act on her own. She asked Mr. Pumariega to come to Posadorio. He was a buyer of real estate. Now she wanted him to look at her property.

When he arrived, she got right down to business. Of course, she didn't tell him the *reason* she wanted the money. All she said was that she needed as much cash as she could get. She wanted to sell everything—the house, the cornfield, the meadow, the woods, the furniture.

Finally, after talking for a long time, Mr. Pumariega told her what he would pay. Doña Berta felt her heart jump with joy. She didn't think that her rundown lands would be worth so much.

Three days later, Mr. Pumariega was in Posadorio again. This time he had some papers for her to sign. Soon everything was settled. Doña Berta put all her money into the little box that held her old secrets.

The old woman fully understood that she was saying good-bye forever to Posadorio, to Aren, to everything. Yes, she was losing everything. But she was going to pay her son's debts! She would buy the painting—and then die of hunger, if she had to.

And what about Sabelona? Mr. Pumariega made it clear that Sabelona could not stay at Posadorio. Doña Berta thought a bit before asking Sabelona to come along with her. She thought about the money. She would have to keep her expenses as low as possible.

Doña Berta wasn't sure if her small fortune would be enough. It would cost a lot to pay her son's debt and buy the painting. Sabelona would be another mouth to feed. Everything would cost twice as much. But in the end, Doña Berta decided to take Sabelona to Madrid with her. She would make up the extra cost by cutting down on her own expenses.

But Sabelona did not want to go. Madrid! The train . . . so many people, so many streets . . . Impossible! She had some family living in a nearby county. She said that she would go to live with them.

"Since Sabelona isn't coming, I'll take the cat," thought Doña Berta. But Sabelona didn't like that idea. She thought that the cat would say "no," if it could talk. But Sabelona couldn't take the cat with her. Two more mouths to

feed would be too much for her family.
And the cat could not be left with Mr.
Pumariega, who would never feed it. So
it was decided that the cat would go to
Madrid with Doña Berta.

On their last day at Posadorio, Doña
Berta and Sabelona went through their
usual routine. Sabelona fixed breakfast,
and they ate together. When her eyes fell
on the cat, Sabelona wanted to weep.
"Poor animal!" she thought. "He doesn't
know what's waiting for him!"

After breakfast, Mr. Pumariega
arrived. He would take Doña Berta to the
station. There he would check her bags
for her and put her on the train. In
Madrid, the owner of a cheap boarding
house was waiting for Doña Berta. Mr.
Pumariega had arranged everything.
When the two women saw him, they
burst into tears. They cried for a long
time, locked in each other's arms.

The cat looked at them, surprised. This
was something new to him. Love was
never shown in that house. In spite of
how they felt, they never showed it

openly. Just in case they needed him, the cat brushed against his old ladies' skirts. Then he scowled at Mr. Pumariega.

Before leaving, Doña Berta asked Mr. Pumariega to wait a moment. She went to the top of the hill. For the last time she stopped there to look out at the view. She did not feel that her lands loved *her*. But she loved *them* just the same. Yes, in this world, one loves not only people, but things. The cornfield, the vegetable garden, Posadorio—all were part of her soul.

The birds were chirping. They seemed to be saying, "What do you have to say to us? You are leaving, we are staying. You are crazy, we are not. You are going off to look for a painting of your son. And you are not even sure that he *is* your son. Good-bye, old lady. Good-bye and good luck."

"Good-bye, good-bye," whispered Doña Berta. She wanted to leave quickly, yet still she didn't move.

"Doña Berta, we are going to miss the train!" shouted Mr. Pumariega. To her it sounded as if he were saying, "You are going to miss your hanging."

Days later, Doña Berta stood on a corner in Madrid. Dawn was breaking, and snow was falling. All the doors were closed. She could see only one door that was open. It was that of a café. The square was empty, except for Doña Berta and the snow. For a long time the old lady stood there without moving.

She was going to early morning mass. The church was the only place she was comfortable in the big city. The priest said the same things there that the priest at home said. That was why she went to mass every day. But the reason she went to such an early mass was something else. Madrid, when it was empty, seemed less scary. The streets seemed less dangerous. The trees seemed more like the "real trees" back home.

"I should have died without seeing this," she thought. "I am just a poor old woman from Susacasa. It hurts too much to be away from the grass, the real earth, the real world." Looking at the city, she felt as if she were chewing dust and touching dry earth. She had to stop herself from calling for help. In her heart she wanted to beg someone to take her back to Posadorio. But she didn't. Instead, she bravely walked through the streets, smiling.

If she smiled, she thought, no one would do her any harm. She gave everyone the right of way on the sidewalk. The people of Madrid must have liked the lively old lady who wore silk the color of tobacco. Many of them smiled at her, too. Nobody had robbed her or tried to cheat her. Still, she was afraid. No one could ever guess how hard it was for her. Just to go out on the street every day was a terrible effort.

Doña Berta was afraid of the crowds. But most of all, she was afraid of being run down. She often imagined herself being trampled by horses, crushed by wheels. Every carriage, every cart, seemed like a loose, wild animal about to jump on her.

The trolley looked like a monster to

her. Since she was so hard of hearing, she could barely hear it coming. If a streetcar came from behind her, she saw danger on the faces of the other people. She would jump out of the way quickly. Then she would let the beast pass, turning her face toward it with a smile.

Many people had saved her from danger. More than once they had caught her in their arms and pulled her out of harm's way. At such times, she would ask herself, "Why am I so afraid of people? There are so many good people in Madrid. Many of them have already helped me."

Still, she was sometimes overcome with a mad desire to turn back. Her heart wanted to run away, to find "her people." She yearned to go home to Sabelona and the trees, the meadow and the house. She had lost all sense of distance. It seemed that she had traveled through space to get to Madrid. She thought it might take hundreds of years to get back home.

Doña Berta was truly lost—lost in the big wide world. She thought that there

were too many people on the earth. In
such a crowd, each person lost some
value. The life of this one or that one did
not matter at all. It seemed that everyone else thought so, too. Doña Berta
could see it in the way they met, talked,
and parted from one another forever.

At first, she did not try to do what she
had come to Madrid to do. It was all she
could manage to keep from dying of
disgust. She was afraid she might die of
the cold in her hotel room. Her window
looked out on a dirty alley they called a
"patio." She became sick and was in bed
for eight days. When she got better, she
decided to ask some questions. She left
the house. That is when she began to
know how dangerous the streets really
were.

Soon, Doña Berta was able to find out
something. The painting she was looking
for was in a large building. The
government was keeping it there for the
time being. They were trying to decide
what to do with it. Would it go into a

museum? Or would it be sold to a rich Latin American who might take it out of Spain?

Doña Berta had found out this much—but she did not know the price of the painting. And she still had not been able to see it. The building was closed to the public. Now she was taking the steps necessary in order to see the painting for herself.

That cold, snowy morning was the beginning of an important day for Doña Berta. At last she would have a chance to see the famous painting! She had found out that it was in a room on the outskirts of the city. It was waiting to be moved. She would have to see it that day or maybe never.

To get there, she would have to go through a lot of snow. But that didn't matter. She would take a carriage—no matter what it cost. She was going to see "her son"! But first, she would go to early mass. There she would ask for heaven's help on this important day.

Doña Berta sat in the dark, cold, empty church. She listened to the priest as he said mass. The words sounded wonderful to her, like something from home. When she left the church, she felt brave and ready to fight for her cause. At last she was ready to look for "her son"—and her son's creditors.

She took a carriage to the building where the painting was being kept. With her pass in her hands, she got past the guards at the door. She walked from room to room, chilled to the bone. She heard the sounds of many hammers that were nailing up boxes. At last, she came up to a fat, poorly dressed man. He seemed to be in charge of moving all the works of art. The paintings were being taken away. Most of them had already gone. Hardly any paintings were still hanging on the walls.

The fat man read her card of introduction. He stared at her. She pointed to one ear to show that she was hard of hearing. That made the man scowl. He seemed to think it was a bother to speak in a loud voice for her.

"So you want to see Valencia's painting! Well, you're almost too late, Grandma. In half an hour, it will be on its way to its new home."

"Where is it? Which one is it?" she asked, trembling.

"That one."

The fat man pointed to a large sheet of gray cloth that was lying at his feet.

"That one, that one! But, it's covered up, for heaven's sake! I can't see a thing!" she cried.

The fat man shrugged his shoulders. "Of course not! Paintings aren't meant to be seen unless they're on display. What do you want me to do about it? You should have come sooner."

"I didn't have the pass before. The public was not allowed to come in. The place was closed. . . ."

The fat man said nothing to her. He turned to a group of workmen and gave them orders. Doña Berta looked all around, as if asking for help.

Four men came over to the painting.

They started to pick it up. Doña Berta let out a cry. "Please, gentlemen! Wait a minute!" she begged. With her clawlike fingers, she grabbed the shirt of a blond, pleasant-looking man. "Please! I want to see him! One second! Who knows if I shall ever have him in front of me again!"

The four men stared at the old lady. Then they all started laughing. "She must be crazy," one of them said.

Doña Berta did not cry often. But at those words, she felt two tears come into her eyes. They slid down her cheeks. When the workmen saw the tears, they stopped laughing.

Maybe she was not crazy after all. It might be something else. The blond fellow explained that they were not in charge here. He told her that the picture was not on display anymore. It was being moved. They were taking it to the home of its new owner, a very rich Latin American.

"Yes, I know. That is why I have to see that figure in the middle of it."

"The Captain?"

"Yes, that's right, the Captain. Help me! I left my town, my home, only for this—to see the Captain. If you take the picture away, what will I do? How do I know that I'll be able to get into the new owner's mansion? And what if he takes the painting off to America?"

The workmen said nothing, just like the fat man, who had left the room.

"Listen," said Doña Berta. "This stepladder will do. Yes! If you will only move it a little closer for me. If you would bring the ladder over here, I could climb up. You could hold the painting up, and I could look at it."

"You'll kill yourself, Grandma."

"No, sir. I won't. Back home in the garden, I used to climb up like that to pick fruit. I won't fall. Please! Help me!"

The blond workman felt sorry for her. The others didn't. But they did help her. One of them brought over the stepladder. Doña Berta climbed up five rungs on the ladder while the workmen held the painting up.

Like a dream, she saw the face. It

looked at her with eyes of fear and terror.
It was the face of "her Captain." It was
the same face she had seen so many
years ago. That living face had also been
stained with blood when she had first
seen it at the gate of Posadorio. Yes, it
was "her Captain"—but it also looked
like herself. He looked like a Rondaliego.
It was her son!

Just as the workmen carried the
painting away, Doña Berta fainted. She
slid down the stepladder into the arms
of the pleasant young blond man.

Doña Berta came to very quickly. She
was brought home in the same carriage,
which was waiting for her at the door.
For two days she remained in bed. Then
she started asking questions.

There was no time to lose. She had to
find out where the new owner of the
painting lived. Her plan was to get into
his house and see the painting again.
Then she could talk to the man about
buying it from him.

Doña Berta did not tell anyone that she wanted to buy the painting. She didn't want anyone to know that she had that much money. Of course, she always carried her money with her. She didn't trust the bank. There was only one safe place for the money. She had sewed the paper bills into her clothes.

Doña Berta never read the local newspapers. She had not heard the sad news about the artist. She did not find out until after she met the new owner of the painting. Like the workmen, the new owner thought that she was crazy. But to him her madness was harmless and interesting.

"Imagine!" he would say to his friends. "Just imagine! This woman wants to buy *Valencia's last painting* from me!" Everyone laughed when he talked about the foolish old woman.

It seemed that the artist had died in a little harbor town. He had grown sick that fall as a result of a chill. This was

Valencia's last painting. It was now worth three times what it had been worth when he was alive!

At first Doña Berta did not know any of this. It took some time before she could meet and speak to the rich Latin American. Someone else had told him about her. Being a kind man, he told his servants to let her in. She visited his house many times before she actually met the man.

The painting was hanging on a wall in his private art museum. It had been placed in a gold frame. Now that she had lots of time to look at it, Doña Berta had second thoughts. She began to doubt that the Captain was really her son. The first time this thought had come to her, she felt chills. A cold sweat ran down her spine.

If she didn't believe that the Captain of the painting was her son—what would become of her? She had given up everything! How could she pay the Captain's creditors, if he was not her son?

No! She must not be mistaken.

She went to the Latin American's home as often as she was allowed. The tips she handed out to the servants made it easier for her to get in. Once inside she would stand in front of the painting for hours. Was he or was he not her son? It is he—but no, it isn't he! She could not make up her mind.

She thought about the saints. Even *they* had sometimes had doubts! Yet they stayed true to their faith. She began to feel the joy of faith in doubt. Suddenly it came to her that courage meant giving one's all—not for one's faith, but for *one's doubt*.

From that moment, she was even more determined to get the painting. This was her state of mind when she first met the rich Latin American. On that visit she did not dare to talk about her plan. But the second time, she told him of her longing to buy the painting.

Doña Berta knew how much the state had been willing to pay for the painting.

She had enough to cover that amount. There would even be some money left over to pay her son's debts. She offered to buy the painting. Then she sat in silence and waited for the rich man's answer.

It was then that he told her why the painter had not answered her letter. The young man had gotten sick while on one of his trips. He had died in search of nature's lessons! Since his death, the value of all his paintings had gone up. The painting of "her Captain" was worth three times as much!

The poor old woman cried. The rich man tried to be kind. He told her he could never let the painting go. Even if she had the amount she had offered, he could not take so much from her. He said that it would leave her much too poor. It was impossible!

Doña Berta cried a great deal and begged a great deal. At last she realized that the rich man would not change his mind. Still, she hoped for a miracle. She made up her mind to get blood out of that stone. Somehow she would get tenderness out of that round rock the rich man called a heart.

For the time being, however, she simply went to see the painting every day. Once in a while, she would ask to see *him*, that rich man. Then she would beg him on her knees. The rich man was kind, of course—but he did not change his mind.

Doña Berta came and went. Every day she braved the dangers of the coaches' wheels and the horses' hoofs. Among the Latin American's friends, she became known as a crazy woman. She became a familiar sight to the people on certain streets.

Half of Madrid seemed to know the smiling, lively old woman. She was the one who wore old-fashioned clothes the color of tobacco. She was the one who ran from carriages and horses and hid in doorways.

One afternoon, someone told her that the rich man was leaving Madrid. He was taking his paintings with him! Paler

than ever and nearly crying, she asked
for a last meeting with him. When they
were alone, she told him her secret.

But even her secret made no difference
to him. Suppose the crazy old woman had
actually had a child under such
circumstances? That didn't prove that
her son was the Captain in the painting!

But the rich man did promise one
thing. He said that she could be there
when the painting was being packed. At
that time she could say good-bye forever
to her Captain—her "supposed son." So
Doña Berta said good-bye to the rich man
until the following day. She was fairly
calm. This was not because she was
giving up, but because she still hoped to
win. She was still expecting some kind
of a miracle.

The next morning Doña Berta was at
breakfast. Her landlady started talking
about the one problem they both had. It
was the cat. The landlady could not stand
him. He was dirtying up the house. He
broke glasses and plates. He tore chairs,

curtains, rugs, and clothes. He ate up food that wasn't his.

The landlady said that something would have to be done. Perhaps the cat and Doña Berta should both leave the house. Or perhaps the cat could be locked up somewhere. Doña Berta finally agreed to lock up the cat—but just for this one important day. She would figure out a better plan later. For now the cat was locked up in the attic storeroom. The iron bars of the skylight were covered with a wire netting. Nobody could hear him from there, even if he turned into a roaring tiger.

Doña Berta left the house. She was sad, angry, and upset about the cat. The slippery ground was polished by the frost. It was early. She had time to spare. She went to church and heard two masses. Finally, the time came. She crossed one street, pushing her way through the crowd. Then came the hard part—crossing Alcalá Street. It took her half an hour to get up her courage. At

last, lifting her skirt slightly, she began
to run across the street.

When she reached Montera Street, she
walked slowly. Now she was getting
tired. She crossed a busy intersection.
Then she entered Fuencarral Street. She
passed in front of a large old house. A
few days before she had met the man who
lived there. "I believe Mr. Cánovas might
help me. Maybe he could make a miracle
happen. He could write a note to force
the Latin American to sell the painting.
Mr. Cánovas has a lot of power. And that
is what power should be used for—to do
good things not covered by law."

While she was thinking about these
things, she wasn't watching where she
was going. At that moment she heard
loud voices. She saw hands reaching out
to her. She felt a blow in the back. Then
something was stepping on her skirt.

"The trolley!" she thought. It was too
late. Yes, it was the trolley. A horse
knocked her down and stepped on her. A
wheel passed over the middle of her body.
The trolley stopped. She had to be pulled

out very carefully from between the wheels. The poor old woman seemed to be beyond help. In 10 minutes, she was dead.

There was only one red stain. A few drops of blood trickled from the corner of her thin white lips. People in the crowd around her felt very sorry for what had happened. But within a few minutes, the body was removed and traffic was back to normal. Thus came to an end the last Rondaliego, Doña Berta of Posadorio.

On Tetuán Street, in a corner of a storeroom, a cat howled. The animal had no name. At one time, it had been a happy creature. It had been a hunter of field mice. It had loved butterflies and naps. Now, forgotten by the world, the cat lived for many days. On its last day, the animal threw itself against the walls. Finally, it dropped into a corner and died. Perhaps it was dreaming of butterflies and "the river" of Susacasa.

Adios, Cordera!

Do city people and country
people have just the same
values? This touching story
is set 100 years ago in rural
Spain. How are two peasant
children affected when the
"march of progress" invades
their meadow?

To Rosa and Pinin, the railway and the telegraph represented the outside world.

Adios, Cordera!

They were three—always the same three—Rosa, Pinin, and "La Cordera."

The meadow was a patch of green spread out like a carpet at the foot of the hill. At one end of the meadow was a railroad track. It led from Oviedo to Gijón. At the other end was a telegraph post that stood like a flag pole. To Rosa and Pinin, the railway and the telegraph represented the outside world. Somehow the children were sure that the unknown world outside of the meadow was a dangerous place.

Pinin would sometimes climb the

telegraph post. He never went all the way to the wires, however. He felt safe only when he had slid down again and planted his feet on the green ground.

Rosa was not as bold as her brother. She was happy just to sit beneath the telegraph post. There she would listen for hours to the wind as it vibrated in the wires. At times the sounds in the wires were like music. Other times, they were whispers traveling from one unknown to another. Rosa didn't care what people on opposite sides of the world were saying to one another. She only liked the sound for its melody and mystery.

"La Cordera" was a cow who had seen much of life. She looked at the telegraph post from a distance. Her only thought was that it was something to rub against. For hours at a time, she lay in the meadow. She passed much of her time just thinking about the peacefulness of life, the gray sky, the quiet earth. She enjoyed trying to improve her mind.

"La Cordera" often played with the children, whose job it was to guard her. If she could, she would have smiled at the idea. How strange that Rosa and Pinin were charged with her care! They were supposed to keep her away from the railroad track. They were to make sure she didn't jump the fence. As if she would even think about jumping the fence! And why would she meddle with the railroad track?

It was her pleasure to graze quietly in the meadow. She could select the best morsels of food easily. Then she would lie down to think. Sometimes she was just happy not to be suffering. Only to exist—that was all that "La Cordera" cared to do.

Other things were too dangerous. Her peace of mind had been shaken when the railway was first put in. She had been almost beside herself with terror when the first train passed. That day she had jumped the stone wall into the neighbor's field. Her fear had lasted for several days. She felt it every single time the train went by.

Little by little she came to know that the train was harmless. After a while, she was able to gaze at the train without even getting up. Finally, she didn't even look up when the train rattled past.

Rosa and Pinin were much more interested in the railway. At first, it brought excitement mixed with dread. When a train would go by, the children would dance wildly about and give out loud shrieks. Then they started to watch the train quietly. Several times a day they would only glance up as the huge iron snake glided rapidly by.

But the railway and the telegraph were not as interesting as the meadow itself. The children's real world was the sea of solitude that surrounded the meadow. There, no living being was to be seen, and no sound from the outside world could be heard.

The children were as close as the two halves of a green fruit. Their love for each other was extended to "La Cordera," the motherly brown cow. She showed great patience when they played roughly with her. No matter what they did she always seemed to enjoy their company.

The children's father, Anton de Chinta, had bought the meadow not long ago. Only since then had "La Cordera" enjoyed such a fine, delicious pasture. Before this, she had to look for food along the public roads.

In those times of poverty, Pinin and Rosa had always tried to find the best spots for her. They tried to protect her from the hardships that animals suffer when they look for food on public land.

Then the cow's calf was born. That brought up a question about her milk. How much should the Chintas have, and how much should go to the calf? Pinin and Rosa always took sides with "La Cordera."

When they could, they would secretly let loose the young calf. The little animal would wildly romp with delight. Then she would rush to seek food and shelter under the body of her mother. The mother would slowly turn her head toward the children. They thought they could see a look of thanks in her eyes.

Such ties could never be broken. Such memories could never be forgotten.

Anton de Chinta had recently decided that he was an unlucky man. Having bought the one cow, he was unable to buy a second one. And he was behind in his rent. He saw "La Cordera" as his only way to raise money. Even though she was like one of the family, the time had come for her to be sold. He remembered his wife's last words. With her last breath she had told him never to sell the cow.

As the mother lay dying, she had turned her eyes toward "La Cordera." It seemed that she was silently asking the cow to be a second mother to the children. "La Cordera" would have to give that affection which the father could not understand.

Anton de Chinta said nothing to the children about needing to sell the cow. One Saturday morning he left at daybreak, before the children woke up.

As he walked down the road, he drove "La Cordera" before him.

When the children awoke, they were confused. They could not explain their father's sudden departure. But they were sure that the cow had gone with him against her will. Then the father brought the cow back that evening. Tired and dusty, he did not explain what had happened. But the children were aware that "La Cordera" was in danger.

The cow had not been sold. The father had set the price too high. The truth was that he really did not want to sell her. He had done this on purpose. That way, he could almost talk himself into believing that he had been willing to sell the cow.

From that day on, Rosa and Pinin had no peace of mind at all. Their worst fears came true when the landlord came to their house. He said they would have to pay the rent or leave.

"La Cordera" now *had* to be sold—even if she brought a low price.

The following Saturday, Pinin went

along with his father. Soon they arrived at a neighboring market-town. Pinin looked with horror at the butchers. He saw that they were armed with weapons of slaughter. To one of these butchers the animal was sold. After being branded, "La Cordera" was driven back to her stable. The bell on her neck tinkled sadly all the way.

Anton was silent. The eyes of the boy were red and swollen. And Rosa, upon hearing of the sale, put her arms around the cow's neck and sobbed.

The next few days were sad ones in the meadow. "La Cordera" did not know what was going to happen. She was just as content as before. But Pinin and Rosa could do nothing but lie on the grass. All of their thoughts about the future were very sad.

Now they looked with hatred at the telegraph wires and the passing trains. These things were connected with the outside world. And that world was robbing them of their only friend and companion.

A few days later, the butcher came with the money. Anton invited him to drink some wine. Then the butcher had to listen to Anton talk about what a special cow this was. The father could not believe that "La Cordera" was not going to another loving master. He wanted to think that she would be well-treated and happy.

Anton kept talking about how much milk she could give. He went on and on about how strong she was with a plow. The other man only smiled as he thought about his plans for the cow.

Pinin and Rosa held each other's hands. They stood watching the enemy from across the yard. Then, as "La Cordera" was being led away, they threw themselves on her neck. They covered her head with kisses.

For some distance they walked along the road with the cow and her new owner. Finally, they stopped and just stood watching. At last "La Cordera" disappeared in the shadows of the bordering hedges.

Their foster mother was lost to them forever.

"Adios, Cordera!" cried Rosa, bursting into tears.

"Adios, Cordera," repeated Pinin, in a breaking voice. "Adios," answered sadly and for the last time the distant cowbell.

Early the following day, Pinin and Rosa went to the meadow. Never had it seemed so quiet. Never had it seemed such a desert waste until now. They could do nothing but lie stretched out on the grass. They were too sad to talk.

Suddenly smoke appeared at the mouth of the tunnel. Then the train came by. In a boxlike car, through narrow windows, they could see the shapes of closely packed cattle.

"They are taking her to the slaughter!" The children shook their fists at the train.

"Adios, Cordera!"

"Adios, Cordera!"

Pinin and Rosa looked with hatred on the railway and the telegraph. They were symbols of the cruel world. And now that cruel world was taking away their companion of so many years just to satisfy its greedy appetite.

"Adios, Cordera!"

"Adios, Cordera!"

Thinking About
the Stories

Doña Berta

1. In what town, city, or country does this story take place? Is the location important to the story? Why or why not?

2. Did the story plot change direction at any point? Explain the turning point of the story.

3. All stories fit into one or more categories. Is this story serious or funny? Would you call it an adventure, a love story, or a mystery? Is it a character study? Or is it simply a picture the author has painted of a certain time and place? Explain your thinking.

Adios, Cordera!

1. An author builds the plot around the conflict in a story. In this story, what forces or characters are struggling against each other? How is the conflict finally resolved?

2. Suppose that this story was the first chapter in a book of many chapters. What would happen next?

3. Good writing always has an effect on the reader. How did you feel when you finished reading this story? Were you surprised, horrified, amused, sad, touched, or inspired? What elements in the story made you feel that way?

Thinking About
the Book

1. Choose your favorite illustration in this book. Use this picture as a springboard to write a new story. Give the characters different names. Begin your story with something they are saying or thinking.

2. Compare the stories in this book. Which was the most interesting? Why? In what ways were they alike? In what ways different?

3. Good writers usually write about what they know best. If you wrote a story, what kind of characters would you create? What would be the setting?

Harris County Public Library
Houston, Texas